POOLE POTTERY

Will Farmer

SHIRE PUBLIC

Published in Great Britain in 2011 by Shire Publications Ltd, Midland House, West Way, Botley, Oxford OX2 0PH, United Kingdom.

44-02 23rd Street, Suite 219, Long Island City, NY 11101, USA.

E-mail: shire@shirebooks.co.uk   www.shirebooks.co.uk

A CIP catalogue record for this book is available from the British Library.

Shire Library no. 631.   ISBN-13: 978 0 74780 835 0

Will Farmer has asserted his right under the Copyright, Designs and Patents Act, 1988, to be identified as the author of this book.

Designed by Tony Truscott Designs, Sussex, UK and typeset in Perpetua and Gill Sans. Printed in China through Worldprint Ltd.

11 12 13 14 15   10 9 8 7 6 5 4 3 2 1

COVER IMAGE

A trio of Freeform vases comprising a shape 699 vase in PRP, shape 714 vase in PJB and a shape 689 carafe in YAP pattern, all after designs by Alfred Read and Guy Sydenham.

TITLE PAGE IMAGE

A shape 970 vase in the AX pattern after designs by Truda Carter, *c.* 1930.

CONTENTS PAGE IMAGE

Detail from the Poole Studio plaque shown on page 47, decorated and fired using experimental glaze effects.

ACKNOWLEDGEMENTS

Mr James Miles, Mr John Clarke, Mr John Smart, Mr Clive Bailey, Mr Jack Morrell, Mr John Lejuene, Mr Michael Jeffery of Wolley & Wallis Auctioneers, Fieldings Auctioneers, Mr Andy Richardson, Mrs Doreen Mann, Mrs Sue Brewer and Ivan Woodward.

Shire Publications is supporting the Woodland Trust, the UK's leading woodland conservation charity, by funding the dedication of trees.

CONTENTS

INTRODUCTION

POOLE POTTERY is recognised as among the most important, distinctive and enthusiastically collected pottery of the twentieth century. Over its long history the company has moved effortlessly through changes in taste and style with an almost chameleon-like approach to design. Steeped in history, Poole Pottery is renowned throughout the world for producing innovative and versatile domestic ceramics that have withstood the test of time, while playing host to some of the most distinguished designers of the twentieth century. From its strong foundations in the nineteenth century's industrial and social revolution, Poole Pottery has created a huge array of decorative wares, from the myriad of utilitarian and decorative tiles to bright and bold hollow wares.

While most major pottery manufacturers were located in the heartlands of Staffordshire, Poole Pottery, originally based in Dorset, grew from a combination of natural raw materials, inspired management, talented designers and skilled craftsmen. Its location, miles away from the suffocating 'smoke' and competition of the Potteries, allowed for a relaxed freedom that would be translated onto the surface of the pottery it so beautifully crafted.

Over the years Poole Pottery has drawn inspiration from many historical styles and cultures and experimented with countless decorative processes and techniques to produce a vast body of work which has created a large and dedicated following of collectors. Arts & Crafts, Traditional, Freeform, Studio, Delphis, Atlantis; the list of 'ranges' of ware goes on, establishing decades of inspired designs and creating a fondness and respect among collectors around the world.

The acute awareness of the wider world around them has allowed Poole Pottery to remain at the forefront of commercial design. Like a generational timeline, the company has undergone many changes in style which, while dramatically different, are unified by their quality. For many years the beating heart of the company was the design and manufacture of tiles. However, the experimentation with art wares at the turn of the century marked a new direction for Poole Pottery which would see them confidently through the twentieth century.

Opposite:
A group of
Freeform range
wares after designs
by Alfred Read and
Guy Sydenham,
c. 1954–7.

Original artwork
by Truda Carter,
c. 1930.

A shape 437 vase
in BD pattern after
designs by Truda
Carter, c. 1930.

From the fluid and lustrous wares of the Arts & Crafts period to the inspired Living Glaze range, Poole Pottery has repeatedly placed itself at the heart of commercial ceramic manufacture with a philosophy that owes a great deal to the studio pottery movement.

In recent years the company has fallen on somewhat troubled times with financial issues, closures and takeovers. Today there seems to be a glimmer of hope that it can move into the twenty-first century with new vigour, new owners and new designs, which will sit happily alongside the truly magnificent body of work from the previous hundred years.

A small group of Atlantis wares after designs by Guy Sydenham, c. 1972–4.

EARLY BEGINNINGS – CARTER & COMPANY

OR CENTURIES the area around Poole has been inextricably linked with the production of ceramics, owing to the massive natural deposits of various types of clay. Since the eighteenth century the fine clay of the region has been exported to the Potteries and beyond, to provide the raw materials for the production of fine quality domestic wares.

From small craft concerns to larger, more significant businesses, there has been a long tradition of manufacture in a region keen to make use of the area's natural resources. The development of a more significant pottery in Poole arose from the increasing demands of a rapidly developing nation during the Industrial Revolution. The increasing wealth of the middle and upper-middle classes was demonstrated through their homes, with decoration and interior design used as visual displays of social status. From chimney breast to hall and from rooftop to garden, the design and decoration of a home was an outward presentation of a family's wealth and success.

The natural bed of dark clays in the area north of Poole was found to be ideal material for the manufacture of architectural ceramics such as bricks, tiles, drain pipes and so on. Among the many companies in the region formed to address the needs of the nation, one of the grandest was that of James Walker. Established in 1861, the company proudly traded as T. W. Walker's Patent Encaustic and Mosaic Ornamental Brick and Tile Manufactory. Such a grand title promised great hope! However, the reality was somewhat different from the ambition. Despite the huge demand for decorative building materials and ceramics, James Walker found himself in a precarious financial position on more than one occasion. We can only assume that Walker was possibly not the most accomplished businessman, as during the 1860s both his stock and business were offered for sale at public auction twice. Eventually, in 1873, Walker was declared bankrupt and the works, housed in a large three-storey building were closed.

Jesse Carter, a successful builders' merchant and ironmonger based in Weybridge, Surrey, would have more than likely been aware of Walker's business and its wide range of fashionable products. In 1873, only a few

Opposite:
A circular plaque
with lustre floral
decoration,
c. 1900–18.

9

A Poole Pottery wall plaque formerly attached to the factory, c. 1925.

Above right: Jesse Carter, c. 1880.

months after Walker's declared bankruptcy and the company's closure, Carter purchased the company, buildings and existing stock. Aware of the growing trend for Walker's products and seeing the possibilities that lay in the acquisition, Carter moved his wife and six children to Poole, taking up residence at Percy House, 20 Market Place.

One of his first moves was to retain the services of James Walker to help him run the works. Carter was the first to admit that he had little practical knowledge in the running of a pottery and such help was vital in the development of his new venture. In 1873 Carter formally changed the name to Carter & Company and set out on a journey of discovery that would lead to the creation of one of the most successful potteries in the country.

In the early years of the company's rebirth, Carter struggled to compete with his rivals in the region, particularly the Architectural Pottery at Hamworthy. Even so, while many new products brought little reward, Carter was making a steady and strong name for himself as a leading manufacturer of encaustic and mosaic tiles. The opening of a London office and his ever-competitive pricing began to yield a return, and by the 1880s the East Quay works was beginning to take a lead over his competitors. Increasingly the company became famed for its production of glazed architectural faience and decorative tiling with the ever-expanding range of decorative mosaic flooring and dramatic advertising panels. Soon major names such as Wedgwood were beginning to feel the pinch of Carter's competitiveness, with many agents complaining that they couldn't buy tiles cheaper than Carter was selling them!

Carter's books began to swell with orders for the wide variety of tiling schemes, from plain geometric designs to his more detailed, even elaborate, pictorial mural panels. Little is recorded or known of the artists decorating these; however, their popularity proved fundamentally important in the development of the company and the increasing interest in more decorative wares against the simpler architectural pieces.

By the 1890s Carter employed Edwin Page, together with his half-brother James Radley Young, both of whom were to prove instrumental in the future of the company's expansion into the domestic and art market. A run of awards and a growing recognition of the company's quality and level of design marked the dawn of a new era. In 1895, their market position and continued march on the competition was finally consolidated with the acquisition of Carter's nearest and largest rival, the Architectural Pottery Company, together with the ultramarine blue manufacturers across the road. This massive merger marked the arrival of Carter & Company as a major if not leading force in the field of architectural and decorative ceramics, even against such massive luminaries as Doulton, Maw & Co. and Wedgwood.

By 1901 Jesse Carter moved to retire, and upon doing so handed the control of the company to two of his sons, Charles and Owen. Charles was the managerial type while Owen was more of a hands-on artist. The brothers, together with their senior designer and potter James Radley Young, continued to develop the factory's output, moving slowly towards an increasing catalogue of decorative wares. No doubt aware of the increasing fortunes of the Doulton Lambeth Pottery in association with the Lambeth School of Art, it was Owen who was to steer the company in a new direction.

Owen had spent a great deal of time on the development and experimentation of decorative glazes, particularly lustre, no doubt influenced by the increasing fashion for such wares prevalent across the industry. From William De Morgan to Pilkington's the magical iridescence of lustre glazes was the epitome of style and fashion. Together with specially appointed glaze technician Alfred Easton, Owen developed a range of decorative lustres that could be applied to their standard stock of tiles or the newly crafted hollow wares of Radley Young.

A range of vases, jugs, dishes and candlesticks was conceived by Owen Carter and James Radley Young and adorned with luxurious glazes in a range of hues from deep red and gold through to green, blue, purple, silver and black. Their creation not only marked the dawn of the new century but also signified a huge change of direction.

A lustre vase by Owen Carter, c. 1900–18.

A lustre wave rim plaque with lustre floral decoration, c. 1900–18.

New manufacturing developments in the industry saw production time slashed from weeks to days, leading to growth and sales. To cope with demand Carter & Company opted for a Dressler continuous firing oven. It was installed in 1913 to cope with the ever-growing demand for their white tiles destined for hospitals and government buildings throughout Britain. Only the second of its type installed in this country, it showed the progressive entrepreneurial style of management displayed by the Carters.

The onset of war in 1914 hit all sectors of industry hard and Carter & Company was no exception. The substantial loss of its workforce led to a huge reduction in their manufacturing abilities, but an ever-inventive Owen Carter and James Radley Young managed to maintain some semblance of normality with the creation of portrait plaques using the Tremblay technique developed at

Wedgwood in the nineteenth century. From political and military leaders to anonymous children, the results were both effective and popular, and maintained a source of income for the factory throughout the course of the conflict.

The war produced many refugees, and among those who settled in Poole was artist Joseph Roelants, who arrived from Belgium in 1914. Together with a number of fellow refugees Roelants began working at Carter & Company where he created a series of tile designs featuring Dutch-inspired scenes, which were exhibited at the 1917 British Industries Fair. The series was created using an in-glaze technique referred to as Delft, a traditional Dutch decorative process that would have been both familiar and natural to him and his fellow refugees. This process was to become an important and distinctive device for the company and while it has been suggested that it was Roelants who introduced

Detail from a relief-moulded charger with lustre glaze by James Radley Young, c. 1900–17.

Right: A Tremblay technique tile back, showing the elaborate company marks.

Above: Lion advertising paperweight, c. 1905–20.

Right: A hand-thrown unglazed vase of compressed ovoid form with painted decoration in the Egyptian and Moorish style, after designs by James Radley Young, c. 1914.

it to Poole, it is more likely that Alfred Easton brought the process with him from his time at Minton.

The decline in popularity of lustre wares saw the need to move towards a new style and taste. Radley Young's passion for potting had seen the creation of a new range of wares which were to become the foundation of what would become the 'Poole style'. In the earlier pre-war years Radley Young had begun creating a range of hand-thrown vessels inspired by forms from ancient history, drawing influence from Egyptian, Moorish and Mediterranean sources. They were simple forms decorated with uncomplicated repeat patterns in brown manganese glazes, often left raw and unglazed to the exterior giving an air of handcrafted antiquity.

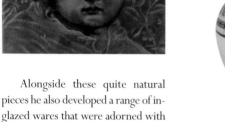

Far left: A Tremblay technique tile depicting Evelyn Shephard, c. 1910.

Left: A tin-glazed vase decorated after designs by James Radley Young, c. 1915–21.

Alongside these quite natural pieces he also developed a range of in-glazed wares that were adorned with simple floral sprig motifs or vertical blue lines, known as Blue Stripe Ware.

This new-found direction was further enhanced with a brief yet significant collaboration with the artists from the Bloomsbury group. Carter & Company were approached by Roger Fry and his fellow artists of the Omega workshops to help them develop a range of ornamental ceramics. Fry, together with Duncan Grant and Vanessa Bell all came to Poole to turn their hand to potting. The results were varied and few; nevertheless, the pieces created a 'buzz' and sense of freedom that was to leave a lasting impression on the studio.

A hand-thrown unglazed vase of ovoid form with twin handles and painted decoration in the Egyptian and Moorish style after designs by James Radley Young, c. 1914.

GOLDEN
YELLOW

SALMON

PALE FRENCH GREY

M BURNT SIENNA
PALE FRENCH GREY

PALE BLACK

FRENCH GREY

REEN

CARTER, STABLER & ADAMS
– DECO DELIGHTS

THE DEATH of Owen Carter in 1919 was to have a deep effect on everyone. A driven and influential character, Owen had been largely responsible for the company's new direction, growing fortunes and position to date. The management of the company fell on the shoulders of Charles Carter, who, while perfectly able, lacked his brother's creative flair.

Over the years Owen had begun moving the company towards the production and manufacture of more decorative wares, consequently causing their market position to grow. The increasing demand for their finely potted wares made common sense commercially and Charles continued to follow this route with the help of his son, Cyril. Cyril had initially started working as a representative for the firm out of the London office, which by 1911 had been firmly established on the Albert Embankment. After his military service Cyril returned to the Poole works to manage the tile works, before moving over to the ornamental department.

Despite the sudden loss of Owen, the company issued its first formal catalogue in 1920. Alongside an introduction from the critic Joseph Thorp, was a selection of illustrations showing wares decorated with floral sprigs or simple repeat banded patterns. The catalogue clearly set out their intention with the promise to produce quality handcrafted wares, each unique in their manufacture. This bold declaration, while easy, required leadership, something Charles felt ill-prepared to provide. Charles saw a solution to his problem in Harold Stabler, a well-respected designer, craftsman and silversmith, who was also the husband of potter Phoebe Stabler. Having risen to prominence through the Arts & Crafts Movement, Harold was now a leading light in the field of design, becoming a lecturer both at the Royal College of Art and later, the Sir John Cass Technical Institute.

Harold in turn encouraged Stoke-on-Trent born potter John Adams to join them. He had spent his early career working in the heart of the pottery industry, both in the tile sector and at Bernard Moore's as a decorator of lustre wares. This was a new start and an exciting opportunity for Adams, who had returned from South Africa having spent time teaching and developing a pottery

Opposite: Original artwork for the Bush-Velt vase by John Adams, c. 1927. The vase made from this design can be seen on page 27.

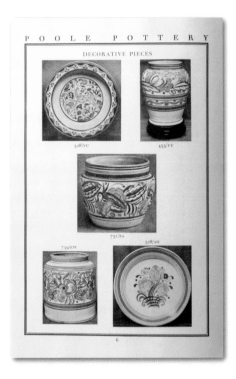

Above:
A Carter, Stabler
& Adams Ltd Poole
Pottery trade
catalogue No 5.

Above right:
A plate from a
Carter, Stabler
& Adams Ltd Poole
Pottery trade
catalogue No 5
illustrated plate.

A Carter, Stabler
& Adams Ltd
impressed mark.

department within the School of Art at Durban Technical College. Together their links in the field of design and industry and skills as designers were to prove invaluable and over the coming years they would play a significant role in the promotion and development of Poole Pottery, the company.

In 1921 Carter, Stabler & Adams was formed as a subsidiary company to Carter & Company with the key objectives of developing and expanding the business from the foundations laid down by Owen Carter and James Radley Young. The structure of the new partnership saw John Adams made Managing Director (although his role was really design and development), the managerial aspects were undertaken by the enthusiastic Cyril Carter, while Harold Stabler's role was a more sideline position acting as an external consultant. While on paper it was a three-way partnership, in truth it was a marriage of five, which was to mark the actual strength of success, as Harold and John's wives – Phoebe and Truda – were to prove as significant to the future of the company as their husbands.

Phoebe Stabler was a recognised sculptress, modeller and designer in her own right having exhibited throughout Britain in many craft and decorative art exhibitions. She brought with her a number of designs which had been modelled and manufactured in her earlier years and these were hastily put into production to be shown at the British Industries Fair of 1921. These new wares were to prove a welcome addition to the existing body of work and drew favourable comment from the critics.

The various figures and relief moulded panels such as 'Spring' and its companion 'Summer' were decorated in the fresh and vivid Della Robbia style, and brought a splash of colour to the displays. Soon further existing designs by the Stablers were included within the range, including 'The Lavender Woman', 'Picardy Peasant', 'Buster Boy' and 'The Bull', which was designed jointly by Harold and Phoebe. Further figures were added, including one of Harold's most significant designs, 'The Galleon'. Introduced in 1925, it was to become an unofficial adopted symbol of the firm throughout the 1920s and 1930s.

A stoneware clay model titled 'The Bull' designed by Harold and Phoebe Stabler, c. 1914.

An oval 'Spring' pattern medallion in glazed Della Robbia colours after designs by Harold Stabler, c. 1921.

Truda Carter's contribution to the company was to be among the most impressive, both in terms of quality and quantity, through some of the most dramatic creations of the 1920s and 1930s. While these designs were to become the trademark 'Poole style' they took some years to develop. The first few years of the new partnership saw the continued production of the existing ranges, particularly the extensive designs of James Radley Young together with the newly introduced figural works of the Stablers. Truda, however, set about modifying the designs, breathing new life into the patterns.

Despite being a highly talented designer in her own right, Truda Carter was never promoted like her competitors Clarice Cliff or Susie Cooper. This may have been due to her own preference, possibly because she was one to avoid the limelight (she was known to have been somewhat reclusive, and even today, very little is known about her personal life). As a result there is very little mention of her in the trade press and commercial journals of the day. Even so, her work featured regularly, and was hailed as a shining example of the new art form, which was steeped in praise.

The year 1922 saw the introduction of not only a new type of body but also a new glaze. A red earthenware clay was

Above: A shape 949 13-inch vase in the LC pattern after designs by Truda Carter, c. 1930.

Above right: A 16-inch shape 946 vase decorated in the HX pattern by Ruth Pavely after designs by Truda Carter, c. 1929–34.

Two 14-inch shape 916 vases in pattern E and F, decorated by Ruth Pavely after designs by Truda Carter, c. 1929–34.

decorated with a semi-matt grey-tinted glaze, which in turn was replaced a few years later with a white slip and cleaner glaze. These formed a more suitable base for the countless new patterns that were becoming bolder, freer and altogether more confident. Simple sprigs and subtle borders were gradually making way for much more elaborate and larger blooms, taking up a greater proportion of the body of the piece.

A shape 947 vase in pattern YE, decorated by Ruth Pavely after designs by Truda Carter, c. 1930.

An original press photograph showing the paintresses in the decorating studio, c. 1930.

A dish-form charger in the GPR pattern after designs by Truda Carter, c. 1930–2.

A colour plate from Seguy's *Suggestions pour etoffes et tapis. 60 motifs en couleur*, c. 1927–8.

Between 1924 and 1927 Poole Pottery participated and was featured in a number of major international exhibitions including the British Empire Exhibition at Wembley, the Paris Exhibition of 1925 (where it was awarded a Diploma of Honour) and the Leipzig International Exhibition of 1927. Following the success of the 1925 Paris Exhibition, Carter, Stabler & Adams developed the practice of public exhibitions both on a national and international level. Exhibitions in London at Heal's Mansard Gallery and regular trade events at the Gieve Gallery in Old Bond Street only enhanced the company's reputation for quality handcrafted wares. Be it home or abroad, the wares displayed met with favourable attention particularly from the trade press who were quick to praise the quality craftsmanship and broad range with countless column inches, supported with numerous illustrations.

The growing international reputation of Poole Pottery was in no small part down to the inventive managerial skills of Cyril Carter, whose constant focus was the continued maintenance of its repute via his many contacts in the design and retail worlds. However, the key figures remained John Adams and his former wife Truda (by now re-married to Cyril Carter). Adams's continued development of shapes and glazes perfectly complemented her work. Her expanding design book was steadily taking the company towards a position as a leading British exponent of the 'new' style.

Never was this illustrated more than through the lavish sales catalogue of 1930, the final and most comprehensive of all the illustrated booklets produced over the period. From the *Studio Year Book* to *The Pottery Gazette*, critics were quick to praise the efforts of this progressive company. A report in *The Pottery Gazette* of 1929 declared:

… its object is to bridge the gulf that lies between the productions of the studio potter and the mass-production factories. A complete range of samples needs to be seen to appreciate what has been achieved within the last generation at the Poole Pottery.

The development of the decorating shop was noted as a significant factor in Poole Pottery's growing fortunes. The early team developed by Radley Young, including Anne Hatchard and Cissie Collett, was expanded to include key artists such as Margaret Holder and Ruth Pavely. By the early 1930s there were over thirty dedicated paintresses working on what we now know as 'traditional' wares. With a strong team and a definite sense of direction, Truda Carter began to grow in confidence.

While responding to the consumers' hunger for a more daring and European style, she remained acutely aware of her competitors. Her work evoked a pure understanding of the new mood in decorative arts that was making its way across Europe following the Paris Exhibition of 1925. The dramatic new

A shape 916 vase in the AW design decorated by Ruth Pavely after designs by Truda Carter, inspired from Seguy's original artwork.

styles and designs on display proved to be extremely influential and were taken up by many of the contemporary potteries who returned home to begin incorporating bold motifs of zigzags, chevrons, triangles and sunbursts, together with stylised animals and female forms.

In recent years, a great deal of research and original source material has shown how both Clarice Cliff and Susie Cooper were influenced by cubism and abstract art. Sadly, by comparison, very little attention has been paid to Truda Carter's designs, even though it seems obvious that embroidery, which she studied at the Royal College of Art, was the dominant influence. She had an excellent knowledge of the Tudor and Jacobean traditions and there can be little doubt that this was the starting point of her unique achievements. Other influences were Radley Young, whose work Truda had so freely adapted and interpreted in her own style, and Vanessa Bell of the Omega workshops.

Nevertheless it was the dramatic designs of the emerging French school of artists that bear most similarities to her designs. Artists such as René Buthaud, Eugene Alain Seguy and Madame Raisin created bold florid and abstract patterns to adorn ceramics, walls and fabrics. It is likely that Truda Carter would have

A shape **966** vase in the KN pattern after designs by Truda Carter, inspired by fabric designs by Mme Charlotte Raisin, c. 1930–4.

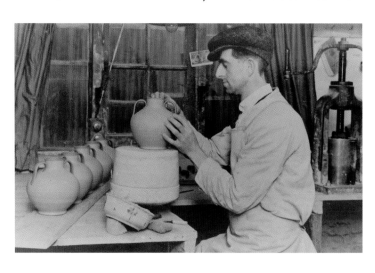

An original press photograph showing a potter creating the shape **202** vase, c. 1930–4.

encountered these on her many travels around Europe, in exhibitions and leaping from the pages of popular periodicals of the day. The designs that emerged from her imagination remain some of the most dramatic, labour-intensive and complicated patterns Poole Pottery ever produced.

Truda would often experiment with a pattern, producing a series of alternate colourways to expand the range. The background colours were also adapted, with pale pink or even grey being used as the base colour. By the early 1930s the base body of the pots had also been developed, being replaced with white earthenware; this in turn transformed the wares from a softer, 'craft' product to something altogether more contemporary and in keeping with the streamlined styling prevalent in the industry.

Soon blousy florals made way for angular abstracts with wheels, cogs and lightning flashes. However, these time-consuming and daring abstract designs were made in far smaller quantities than the everyday wares which were relied on for survival. The larger abstract pieces served as important promotional wares for exhibitions and advertising, showing the ever-astute buying

A large shallow dish-form wall plaque, decorated in the HX pattern after designs by Truda Carter, c. 1929–34.

Original artwork for the HX pattern wall plaque by Truda Carter, c. 1929.

public that Poole Pottery was a firm who were 'on trend' and 'in vogue', but they are a far cry from the many thousands of preserve pots, biscuit barrels and bowls that were snapped up on a daily basis in department stores and china shops. These more significant pieces also became inspirational starting points for the more mass-produced designs of the period, allowing a style to permeate through the whole production at the workshops.

While the work of in-house designers was the mainstay of the factory's output, the 1920s and 1930s saw the addition of guest designers contributing to the growing design books. Harold Stabler was a great

A circular dish-form plate decorated in the CM pattern known as 'Sugar for the Birds' after designs by Olive Bourne, c. 1926–7.

Original artwork for the CM pattern by Olive Bourne, c. 1926.

instigator of designs from external artists and Charles Carter was also quick
to persuade various graduates of the Royal College of Art to contribute.
Erna Manners was one of the first to be invited, producing the Grape and
Fuchsia (which became one of the most popular patterns ever produced).
Olive Bourne developed a series of figural and portrait designs including a
pattern now affectionately known as 'Sugar for the Birds', which showed a
stylised female among flowers and foliage holding a treat for a small bird.
This design, along with a pattern now called 'The Leipzig Girl', took pride
of place at the Poole Pottery stand at the Leipzig Internal Exhibition of
Industrial Art in 1927. Figural work from Harold Brownsword and Hugh
Llewellyn also expanded the range, giving a wide and varied feel to the
company's already impressive catalogue of designs.

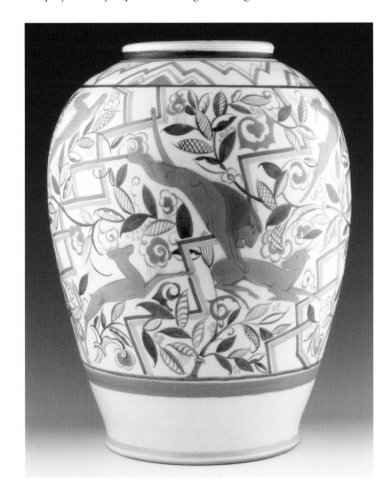

A shape 946 vase
in the LZ or Bush-
Velt pattern after
designs by John
Adams, decorated
by Ruth Pavely,
c. 1927–34.

An Everest Ware conical stepped bowl designed by John Adams, c. 1930–3.

While Truda's patterns epitomised the mood in surface decoration, John Adams's love of shape and form was to be equally successful in interpreting the prevailing Art Deco style. Between 1930 and 1933 the Everest, Plane and Picotee ranges were introduced, which relied on nothing more than angular forms, graduated bands and graded colour palettes for impact. Pure minimalism, they were stylish statement pieces that made perfect use of the newly developed glaze effects. The introduction of these simple elegant forms paved the way for one of Poole Pottery's most important new ranges, Streamline, developed by John Adams and Ernest Baggaley in 1935–6.

As John Adams developed the shape, Ernest Baggaley worked on a new Vellum semi-matt glaze that could be produced in a wide range of new colours. This new glaze was significant in its durable and watertight qualities, key attributes for everyday domestic wares. Suddenly the company had a large and standardised range that was quick and relatively cheap to produce, while at the same time was immensely popular with consumers.

A Plane Ware vase of cylindrical form designed by John Adams, c. 1930–3.

Poole Pottery grew at an exceptional rate with additional Dressler ovens installed to service the growing demand for the new fashionable wares, and the factory felt vibrant and alive with an expanding pattern book that sought to capitalise on Baggaley's new glazes. Figures, wall pockets and all manner of ornaments were produced in massive quantities to service the lower end of the market, setting a strong foundation for future growth and development.

A pair of model 813 Elephant bookends designed by Harold Brownsword, c. 1928–30.

A model 831 Springbok table lamp designed by John Adams, c. 1930.

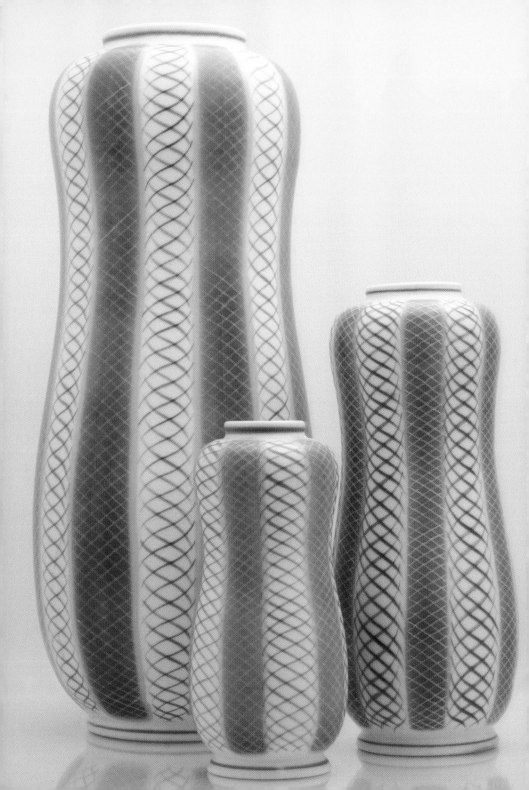

THE FREEFORM YEARS

FOR THE DURATION of the war, like many firms producing and supplying the luxury goods market, Carter, Stabler & Adams was reduced to a virtual standstill operating with only a skeleton staff as restrictions were put in place limiting the manufacturing abilities of most companies. The factory buildings were turned over to storage facilities or office space, the showrooms were taken over by Imperial Airways and the old bottle kilns were acquisitioned as air raid shelters, putting the near derelict site to good use for the local community.

Unlike the porcelain manufacturers, who were able to continue manufacturing and trading with the overseas markets, Carter, Stabler & Adams chose to concentrate on the production of functional domestic everyday items and replacement pieces to address the needs of those bombed out by the conflict, and of course, military wares.

Wartime restrictions arose from various advisory committees assembled from many leading lights in the world of design (including Gordon Russell, Alfred Read and Enid Marx), and together they persuaded the Government to enforce a policy of no or minimum decoration, monochrome colour if colour had to be used, and, most importantly, standardisation. The restrictions were intended to unify the industry but in fact they were met with grim acceptance; both manufacturers and the wider general public saw the policy as a further depressing addition to already difficult times.

Carter's answer to these new outline rulings was quite simple, with the continued manufacture of existing products. Adams's Streamline range of 1935–6 sat well with the rulings, and earlier colour ranges were replaced with a simple white glaze, while minor alterations were made to keep the designs fresh and current. Somehow they gracefully survived through these most difficult times, and in a way emerged stronger and leaner than at the start of the war.

The end of the Second World War brought about a period of complete reconstruction and reorganisation, not only of the factory but the future of the company. Staff numbers had considerably dwindled with many skilled workers

Opposite:
A graduated trio of Freeform shape 699, 700 and 702 shape 'Peanut' vases in the PKT pattern after designs by Alfred Read and Guy Sydenham, c. 1953–4.

not returning to their posts, and on a practical side, the factory site and much of its equipment was in desperate need of repair or replacement. Furthermore, many of the key figures responsible for the company's pre-war prosperity were becoming as tired as the buildings that once buzzed with their success. After some thirty years of dedicated service, John Adams was now not a well man, and in 1945 Harold Stabler died and Truda Carter reached retirement age. A number of other important workers including Ernest Baggaley left to set up their own pottery concerns, leaving a massive void for a company that was keen to develop and grow in a time of post-war optimism.

In 1945 Cyril Carter was joined by his son David, together with Roy Holland (who came from the Potteries in Stoke-on-Trent). Holland was

A group of Freeform vases in YMP and YAP patterns after designs by Alfred Read and Guy Sydenham, c. 1953–5.

immediately appointed works manager and was set the sizeable task of rebuilding the East Quay site. Cyril Carter persuaded his fellow board of directors to inject much-needed cash, and between 1946 and 1949 the East Quay works were redeveloped into a modern factory using new production methods and kilns including the installation of a new tunnel kiln.

With the new premises up and running the factory set about making it pay. While still bound by Government restrictions the factory managed to revive some good pre-war overseas relationships with the introduction of their Twintone and Cameo ranges. Their simple yet effective dual-colour glazed bodies were a surprising success, catching the eye of competitors (and imitators) across the industry, and there were more than a few similar designs introduced to the market by other firms. Along with these new 'fashionable' wares the company also revived some staple classics such as the familiar florals of Truda Carter.

In 1949 John Adams finally stepped down from his role as managing director. This was met with great concern for the future of the company as not only had Adams steered its fortunes on a business level, but he also had been in overall control of the artistic direction of the company.

Adams, however, was confident in the abilities of Lucien Myers who had been brought on board to replace him. Myers, while filling the business aspects of the position, needed to find someone to replace Adams's skills as

A Streamline tea and coffee service in Twintone finish after designs by John Adams, c. 1950.

a designer. Myers was a shrewd businessman who brought with him a broad knowledge of the industry following his position as Editor of the trade journal *Pottery Gazette and Glass Trades Review*. Acutely aware of the mood in the industry and the direction in which ceramics were moving, he was keen to adopt the many successful practices of overseas competitors.

In 1950 Claude Smale, a recent young graduate of the Royal College of Art, joined the Poole Pottery as Head of Design with Ruth Pavely as assistant. His immediate task was the design and production of commemorative wares for the 1951 Festival of Britain but various problems surrounding the application for a production licence meant that few pieces were actually manufactured. It was the creation of a number of simple elegant vessels and vases for which he will be most remembered. Inspired by the elegance and simplicity of Scandinavian wares available, pots were hand thrown in white earthenware; their swollen and elegant silhouettes were not only contemporary and 'on trend' but also proved to be the foundation for subsequent ranges. For reasons still seemingly unknown, Smale only stayed for some six months; maybe the position was just a step too far for a young graduate, but whatever the reason, a replacement was needed – someone with greater knowledge and experience.

Alfred Burgess Read was 52 years old when he was appointed Head of Design at Poole Pottery in 1950. A graduate of the Royal College of Art, Read had studied under the late Harold Stabler in the 1920s and in the following

A trio of shape 701 'Peanut' vases in PKT, PLC and PKC patterns after designs by Alfred Read and Guy Sydenham, c. 1953–5.

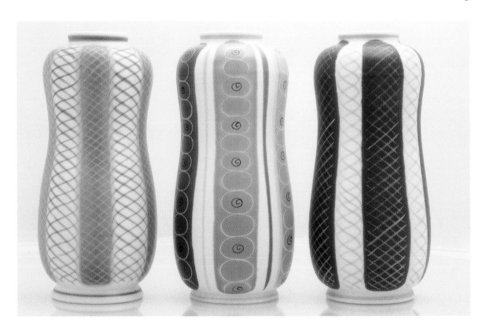

years had built a strong reputation in the industry with a respected and distinguished career under his belt. Although his expertise was in lighting, he was above all a successful and accomplished designer who held the accolade of Royal Designer for Industry. Following her graduation from the Chelsea School of Art, Read's daughter Ann joined the company a year later. Having no formal knowledge or experience in the decoration and manufacture of ceramics, she was placed in the skilful hands of leading artist Ruth Pavely.

Across all industries teams of designers were beginning to reshape a world battered and bruised by conflict and Carter & Company was no different.

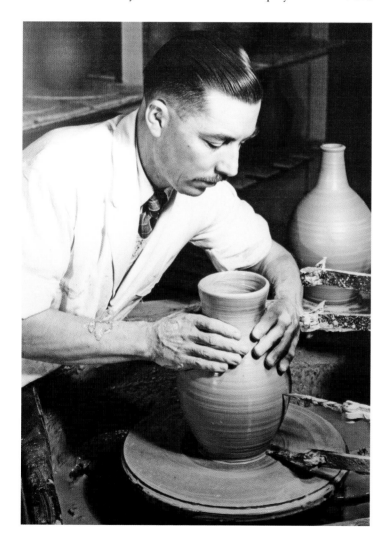

An original publicity photograph of Guy Sydenham at the potter's wheel, c. 1953.

A circular dish-form plate hand-decorated with an image of Guy Sydenham at the potter's wheel, possibly by Anne Read.

A tight and experienced group of designers set about re-inventing the company's products for a hungry new consumer. Alfred Read was the key designer supported by thrower, Guy Sydenham, and he had artists-cum-designers in his daughter Anne, as well as Ruth Pavely. Guy Sydenham had joined Poole Pottery in 1931, completing a seven-year apprenticeship working alongside James Radley Young, John Adams and Truda Carter. The war had interrupted Sydenham's career, but he returned to Poole after military service, initially training apprentices and establishing the new production processes as the factory modernised after the conflict.

With a fresh mood of confidence the team set about experimenting and developing new ranges with a freedom not previously experienced within the industry. Read set about transforming the products including a complete overhaul of the glaze palette, creating a fresh new tone for the new designs together with the introduction of many new shapes following on from the work of Smale. Elegant dishes, bottle vases and gourd forms were among the new shapes introduced, which were, in turn, decorated with characteristically stylish patterns emerging from the period.

With a strong awareness of the greater interior design movement arising around him Read drew inspiration from the many exciting textile and print designs emerging from fellow artists and designers. There was a strong sense of integration and a desire to produce a harmonious environment where pieces seamlessly sat together. Whenever and wherever works were exhibited they were shown alongside panels of contemporary fabric or resting on the latest furniture.

As with all industries imitation is the greatest form of flattery and all too soon these new wares were the subjects of widespread plagiarism. In a move to combat the encroaching march of lesser wares Read simply increased output, constantly developing new patterns to keep the range fresh and exciting and also keeping one step ahead of the competition.

Opposite:
A group of Freeform wares consisting of a 696 vase in PKC pattern, a 651 vase in GBU pattern and a 705 vase in PLC pattern: designs by Alfred Read and Guy Sydenham, c. 1953–4.

While new wares were instrumental to the future success of the company there was still a place for the more traditional designs of the pre-war years. With a proven track record the stylistic floral works of Truda Carter remained popular with the buying public. In keeping with the new mood at the firm these traditional wares were also given an overhaul, resulting in a harder, almost simplified version of the originals. Furthermore, technological advances had resulted in the refining of both the body and the surface glaze with the

introduction of Alpine white was felt to be more in keeping with the 'new look'. These 'refreshed' floral wares found favour around the world, with growing order books from the Americas, Australia and the Far East, to name but a few.

While the factory had been allowed to sell second-rated wares, Government restrictions on the sale of decorated items to the home market were not lifted until 1952. A decade or more of austerity had led to a pent-up demand for wallpapers, fabrics and pottery incorporating bold colours and the latest designs, as a nation turned its back on the dark days of the past.

A Freeform shape 692 vase in PQB pattern, a shape 693 vase in PQC pattern and a shape 694 vase in PJL pattern, all after designs by Alfred Read and Guy Sydenham, c. 1953–4.

Many members of the Second World War advisory panels quietly thought that the paring down of design, quashing of pattern and absence of colour would see the birth of cool, modern and simple wares in the post-war years. However, the exact opposite was actually the case. The years of abstinence had most definitely made the heart grow fonder and in the post-war years the hunger and desire for bold decorated wares was acutely stronger than had been imagined!

The year 1956 saw the formal introduction of the Freeform range. A collaborative product of both Alfred Read and Guy Sydenham, the wares were both ground-breaking and successful. Believed to have been inspired by the sculptural work of Henry Moore and the growing influential movement known as the 'California West Coast look', the various vases, dishes and vessels were pure modernism!

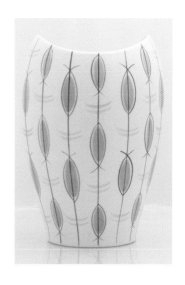

A Freeform shape 720 vase in the PY pattern after designs by Ruth Pavely and Ann Read, c. 1956–7.

A Freeform shape 689 carafe in the HOL pattern and a shape 722 vase in the HOL pattern after designs by Ruth Pavely and Ann Read, c. 1956–7.

In response to the growing catalogue of shapes, surface designs flowed in huge numbers. From simple all-over coloured glazes, which defined the shape and form, to the countless repeat surface patterns, the wares hit the perfect note with the young consumer. Production boomed as the slip cast wares were quickly and deftly decorated by the skilled hands of the Poole workforce.

While the production line continued to manufacture the approved designs the studio proceeded to develop more complex ideas. While not always commercially viable, these highly complex pieces were shown as

Poole Tableware

Contour

Sky Blue and Dove Grey
Mushroom and Sepia
Ice Green and Seagull
Gold on White

Contour combines a classic shape with either Poole's unique soft coloured "vellum" glazes in the Twintone ranges, or with the simplicity of gold banding in Gold on White. With a very wide range of items available, the Contour collection can be purchased piece by piece or as complete sets.

Poole
Poole Pottery Ltd.,
The Quay, Poole, Dorset BH15 1RF

A 1960s original sales leaflet displaying the Contour range.

promotional pieces in exhibitions or trade fairs, and more importantly provided inspiration for the simpler commercial wares. Today these rare pieces are seldom seen, yet represent the purest form of Poole's foray into the new mood in ceramic design.

Despite the runaway success of this new range Alfred Read was to step down just two years later. His retirement marked not the end of an era, however, but the start of a new one. In his place came Robert Jefferson, a product of the new mood in design arising from the teaching principles that the design should fit the purpose like a hand to a glove. A graduate of the Royal College of Art with many years of training and experience, he was more than qualified for a position he had long dreamed of.

A selection of Contour shape tea wares in grey glaze finish after designs by Robert Jefferson, c. 1963.

Under his direction the company's long-held position as a pioneer of modernism and fashionable trends was upheld with a series of bold new developments and ranges. Having addressed many issues regarding the profile and public perception of the company, he set about steering the firm in a new direction. Everything was subject to either a tweak or complete re-design, from promotional material to the showrooms, creating a brand that was both confident and strong.

Jefferson's key strategy was a shift from decorative hollow wares into the booming domestic and tableware market. While building a team of fellow designers around him he began creating various ranges of tea, dinner and table wares that would perfectly suit the manufacturing processes established at the factory. The introduction of the Contour range with its fluid open form marked his formal stamp on the company's product timeline. Sold in a wide range of colours and patterns from the simple Twintone to the critically acclaimed Pebble pattern, the wares were an instant success.

Further tableware ranges followed, including Compact, which addressed the ever-changing needs of new families, while his range of Bokhara storage jars perfectly suited the needs of the modern kitchen. Jefferson was a forward-thinking man who was able to combine the qualities of craft and studio creation with the commercial aspects of mass manufacture. His imaginative yet practical approach to design was to prove significant for future developments at Poole Pottery and marked one of the most diverse and creative periods in the company's history.

POOLE GOES POP

D URING THE 1960s the years of post-war austerity made way for a new age of freedom and prosperity. A new generation arose filled with self-confidence and a belief that anything was possible. From fashion to music, interiors to everyday life, everything was vibrant, new and exciting. Carter & Company was no different with a fresh outlook and its team of inspired artists and designers.

With focus and impetus Jefferson set about developing the Studio, established as a centre of development and experimentation. The ideas dreamt up here would not only show them as a hot bed of design talent but also form the basis for more commercial lines. Over the coming years not one but three new ranges would be developed. This new Studio was arguably one of the most important contributions to the British pottery industry and firmly placed Poole as one of the most, if not the most, forward-thinking potteries of the day.

Jefferson's initial brief was to develop the work of Alfred Read with the creation of new shapes and glazes, wares that would complement and ultimately replace the traditional ones. In 1961, with the help of Guy Sydenham, Jefferson developed a small range of individual pieces that were exhibited at the Tea Centre in Regent Street, London, to launch the new Studio. The new wares were daring and bold, bridging the gap between the studio potter and the commercial factory manufacturer. Heavily inspired by the wider studio movement of the day these new wares reflected the vogue for black and white decoration inspired by the so-called 'Picasettes' (imitators of Picasso) and also the influence of the emerging Op Art movement.

The new range was well received and with a receptive audience it was decided that the Studio and the new range should be expanded and more designers taken on. A vacancy at the Studio was advertised at the Poole Employment Exchange in 1962 with details passed to other employment exchanges around the country. In South Wales the vacancy came to the attention of Tony Morris; and while Morris had no formal experience in the field of ceramic design he was employed on the strength of his artistry and

Opposite:
A large Aegean shape 93 vase with a shape 14 vase decorated with repeat abstract patterns, c. 1970s.

Above: A trio of Studio vase shapes 1, 25 and 27 designed by Robert Jefferson with decoration by Robert Jefferson, Tony Morris and other selected artists, c. 1961–3.

Right: A Studio vase shape 46 designed by Robert Jefferson, c. 1961–3.

painterly skills. Morris's engagement was to prove significant in the cultivation of the new emerging look. His distinctive style and fervent imagination contributed to some of the most exciting and influential pieces while pushing the boundaries of commercial ceramic design.

With a growing team and a sense of purpose new ideas began to flow from the Studio.

Two Studio vases
shapes 9 and 10
designed by
Robert Jefferson
and decorated
with wax resist
glaze work
possibly by Tony
Morris, c. 1961–3.

A trio of Studio
shape 50 bottle
vases decorated
with incised and
wax resist glazed
decoration
possibly by Tony
Morris, c. 1963.

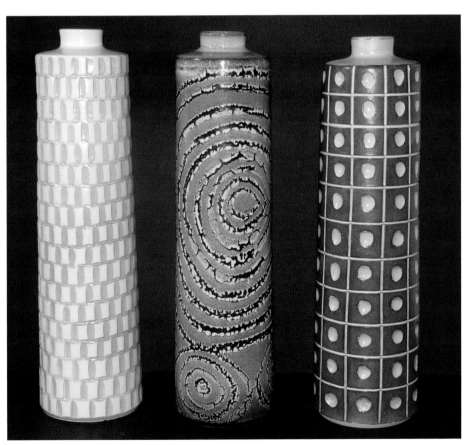

The new range featured a wide array of bowls and vases including all manner of tall cylinders, tapered conical vessels, broad barrel forms and dishes. Often heavily carved or incised with repeat abstract patterns the items were fresh and completely on trend. From nature to industrial influences the decoration was varied, with stylised trees and birds, imaginary faces or even abstracted aerial views of towns and cities. The ethos and philosophy were daring and innovative with a freedom never seen before in the industry.

The early Studio pieces were thrown by Sydenham and decorated by Jefferson, Morris and the team. Using the most expensive glazes and processes, these pieces were unique and exciting but also time-consuming and incredibly expensive to

Above: A unique Studio abstract sculptural piece with carved and glazed decoration possibly by Tony Morris, c. 1975.

Right: A large Studio dish shape 43 with 'Sun Face' decoration designed and decorated by Tony Morris, c. 1963–4.

produce. It is well documented that the final retail cost for a single plate was well in excess of an artist's weekly wage, yet despite this they sold well. That so much time, expense and effort could be afforded was in no small part down to the work of Jefferson and his development of the main commercial lines. His outstanding achievements in creating a stable and secure income stream from the everyday products allowed him and his team this level of creative freedom. While they had found an audience for these new wares there was a more significant purpose to them. Out of the many experiments and trials

A circular Studio charger decorated with abstract horseshoe motifs designed and decorated by Tony Morris, c. 1963–4.

An oval Studio charger decorated with an abstract 'Pollard Tree' designed and decorated by Tony Morris, c. 1962–3.

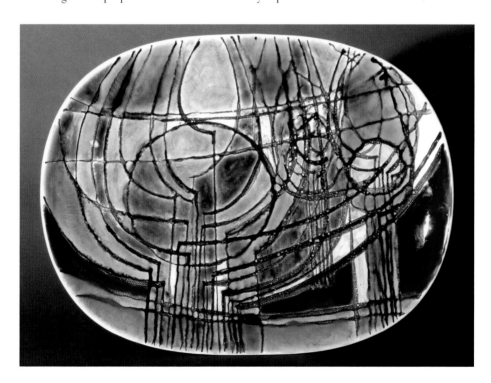

A circular Studio charger decorated with abstract 'Sun Face' motifs designed and decorated by Tony Morris, c. 1963–4.

arose a more commercial product that owes its heritage to the exciting developments of the Studio years.

In 1963, at an exhibition held at Heal's, the prestigious London department store, Sir Gordon Russell launched the Poole Pottery Delphis Collection, which consisted of around seventy-five pieces designed as a standard repeatable range. This allowed trade customers to place orders with a degree of certainty as to size, shape and price and, furthermore, it allowed return customers to re-order from the associated catalogue of designs. Although shapes were standardised, the colour, decoration, glazing and carving of each piece was unique. In simple terms this was a modern industrial manufacturer producing pottery with a handcrafted studio feel on a large commercial scale.

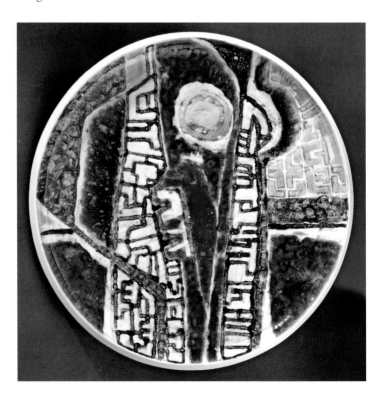

A circular Studio charger decorated with an abstract town plan designed and decorated by Tony Morris, c. 1963–4.

New patterns were later added, and with the growing success paintresses were called in from other departments to assist. Experimentation was the key word with trails on glazes, decorating techniques and surface pattern. Artists were not required to work to a standardised pattern book and there were no boundaries on subject matter. More importantly, no two pieces were the same. In his autobiography Guy Sydenham described this time as a 'vibrant decade ... full of energy and innovation'.

Despite the commercial success of the mainline ranges and the boundless creative flair of the Studio all was not well at management level. In 1963 Lucien Myers, a long-standing advocate and supporter of the artistic side and, more importantly, an immensely successful salesman, resigned. To further compound matters, Cyril Carter, the last remaining member of the Carter dynasty, retired from the board. That these two giants of the business departed within a short space of time, was partly due to the takeover which occurred the following year.

After a year or more of lengthy negotiations Pilkington's took control of the company in 1964. At the time the word 'merger' was used, but the complete transfer of board members in favour of Pilkington's presented a truer sense of the acquisition. Pilkington's was primarily concerned with

Above left: An original artwork for a series of seasonal chargers designed by Tony Morris, c. 1965.

Above: A 16-inch shape 85 Delphis range cylinder vase, c. 1966–9.

A group of small
Delphis range
circular dishes,
c. 1966–9.

A shape 90
Delphis range vase,
c. 1968–72.

the commercially healthier tile side of the business which had been a major competitor to them for many years. However, true to their word they provided a much-needed injection of capital to the domestic and decorative side of the business. There seemed to be an inherent appreciation and understanding of the artistic heritage of the business, Pilkington's having once been a producer of fine art wares. The general re-ordering of the upper management, the departure of Lucien and Cyril and the introduction of a new board with new ideas undoubtedly brought about changes on the factory floor.

To the outward viewer the renamed Poole Pottery Ltd was as strong as ever: growth was assured and progress was undeniable. Nevertheless, years of trust, friendships and working practices were brushed away in a moment. By 1965 it seemed that Robert Jefferson had all but designed himself out of a job and on his departure the role was not filled.

Over the coming year changes by the new management involved an increased investment in equipment, which in turn resulted in additional demands in production. The Studio established by Robert Jefferson was integrated into a re-working of the site that was to include a shop and visitor centre to meet the needs of the increasing numbers of visiting public. Formally opened in May 1966, the newly named Craft Section was created to service the orders for either the standard range or the special orders.

Interior pages from an original sales brochure, c. 1976.

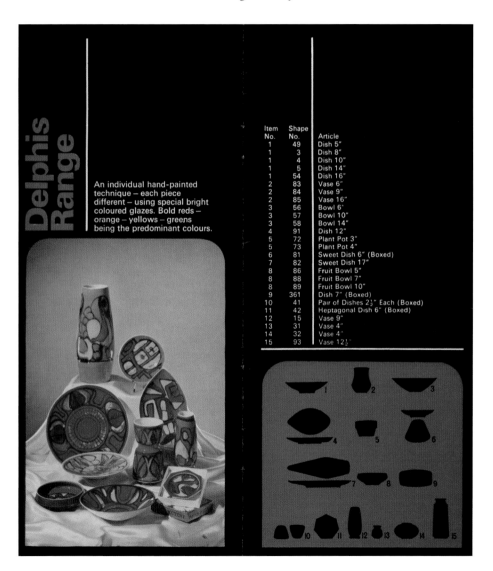

Delphis Range

An individual hand-painted technique – each piece different – using special bright coloured glazes. Bold reds – orange – yellows – greens being the predominant colours.

Item No.	Shape No.	Article
1	49	Dish 5"
1	3	Dish 8"
1	4	Dish 10"
1	5	Dish 14"
1	54	Dish 16"
2	83	Vase 6"
2	84	Vase 9"
2	85	Vase 16"
3	56	Bowl 6"
3	57	Bowl 10"
3	58	Bowl 14"
4	91	Dish 12"
5	72	Plant Pot 3"
5	73	Plant Pot 4"
6	81	Sweet Dish 6" (Boxed)
7	82	Sweet Dish 17"
8	86	Fruit Bowl 5"
8	88	Fruit Bowl 7"
8	89	Fruit Bowl 10"
9	361	Dish 7" (Boxed)
10	41	Pair of Dishes 2½" Each (Boxed)
11	42	Heptagonal Dish 6" (Boxed)
12	15	Vase 9"
13	31	Vase 4"
14	32	Vase 4"
15	93	Vase 12½"

Interior page from an original sales brochure with full range and price list, c. 1972.

In one sense the Studio was the victim of its own success. The marketing and promotion, along with the sheer popularity of the designs and fashionable colour palette, saw it sell not only on home shores but as far afield as Japan, America and Canada. Such was the need to meet the thriving orders that further standardisation was instigated, production was increased and more paintresses were recruited. In 1966 following a visit by Sydenham and Morris to the potteries at Vallauris it was agreed that the red and orange hues should form the foundation of all future Delphis designs in order to address the growing commercial needs of the production line. The wares perfectly complemented the new mood in interior design with the bold, even psychedelic, styling sitting perfectly alongside the latest look in interior design.

Although paintresses were given the freedom to create their own designs, in time financial rather than artistic considerations took precedence. To speed production and in the interests of regularity the number of glazes available was reduced and by 1971 the palette of colours was simplified to predominantly red, yellow, orange and green, which were not only less costly colours but also more stable in the production process. More significantly paintresses were paid according to the number of pieces they produced with a minimum requirement per day; mass production took over from art, and the principles of experimentation and free expression – the cornerstones of the Studio philosophy – were all but lost to the dictates of commercialism. All too soon the Delphis wares were being promoted as 'gift' wares alongside the traditional pieces, indicating that their status had dropped from the earlier

intention of their creator Robert Jefferson.
Despite this, the Delphis range remained a
cornerstone of Poole Pottery's fortunes
and production until its withdrawal
in 1980.

While the Studio wares and
their subsequent transformation
into the popular Delphis range
was the most significant
development of the period, two
further ranges were to become
meaningful in Poole Pottery's
canon of work. In 1970 the
company continued to develop the
craft elements established through the
introduction of the Delphis range. A
natural progression in terms of technique
and manufacture came in the form of the
Aegean range. Developed throughout 1969 it
featured five distinctive decorative techniques: silhouette,
scrafitto, mosaic, flow line and carved. The various techniques were both
inventive and technically accomplished with superb use of modern glazes
and production methods. Initially developed by Leslie Elsden as a
replacement for the Delphis range, it featured abstract, landscape, marine
and animal subjects in a darker palette over a range of some twenty-two
standard shapes. It was never as popular as its more vibrant sibling, but ran
as a complementary rather than replacement range, again until 1980.

An Aegean charger
decorated with a
stylised tree design
possibly by
Diana Davies
from a range
masterminded by
Leslie Elsden,
c. 1970–4.

The creation of the Atlantis range was more in keeping with the
philosophy of Studio pottery and was in some respects the most avant-garde
of the Pottery's commercial output. First introduced by Jefferson in the late
1960s, the range was fully developed by Sydenham over successive years.
This distinctive range was heavily hand-embellished with carved and worked
surface decoration featuring cogs, wheels, zigzags, lines and spots over the
rich red terracotta body with various green and oxide glazes used to enhance
areas of decoration.

This resulted in a distinct marine feel, no doubt influenced by
Sydenham's daily commute to work by boat from his island home in Poole
harbour. The range, which included vases of all shapes and sizes together with
a series of lamps and some other novelty wares, ran successfully till 1979.

Poole Pottery marked its centenary in 1973 followed by a royal visit from
Her Majesty the Queen and Prince Philip in 1979, but these landmark
moments were countered with the retirement in 1976 of Holland,

and more importantly, the departure of Sydenham in 1979. Holland was replaced by Trevor Wright who sparked a new spirit of diversity in the company's production.

The revival of the traditional wares took the hand-painted skills away from the Craft Section. It introduced a new audience to heritage-based wares together with the increasingly growing development of the domestic market. With a wider range of printed table wares the changing trends in the market could quickly be addressed.

A selection of
Atlantis Wares,
c. 1973–6.

Guy Sydenham had fought for years to preserve the integrity of the Studio and to reverse the decision to implement a piece rate at the factory. Feeling that he was fighting a losing battle in the face of commercialism he tendered his resignation, perceiving that his position and desire for creative freedom were untenable. Following his departure, the Craft Section that had been the working heart of the company for nearly twenty years rapidly declined, and was eventually closed in 1982.

This marked the end of one of the greatest creative chapters in the company's history, yet it would appear that while a sad reflection of the status of craft pottery it was a necessary evil for the continued financial success of a firm that had always followed the market around it.

Above: An original press photograph of the bottle kiln made to commemorate the firm's centenary in 1973.

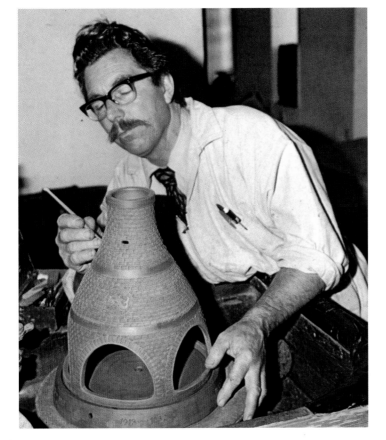

Left: An original press photograph of Guy Sydenham working on the commemorative bottle kiln, c. 1973.

TOWARDS THE NEW CENTURY

THE 1980s saw a period of alteration and adaptation in response to a change in the market and consumer demands. The closure of the Craft Section together with the ensuing depression of the late 1970s and early 1980s meant the company once more needed to change direction in order to survive.

While the traditional wares continued to be a mainstay of production the creative flair of the Studio era was all but gone. It was replaced with a varied array of table and decorative wares, which were not as stimulating or challenging as Studio, Delphis, Atlantis or Aegean, but provided the company with stability, which was far more vital in such challenging times. Like many other potteries across the country, Poole set about a scheme of cost reduction with limitation on ranges and shaving of production costs wherever possible.

In 1982 Tony Morris, one of the last of the Studio team, left, and Alan White took over Guy Sydenham's role. White began creating a new design team that included Alan Clarke, Ros Sommerfelt and Elaine Williamson. They set about introducing new ranges that included a number of transfer printed patterns, which were far less labour-intensive than the hand-painted wares and marked a new direction and look for Poole Pottery.

While glaze-based decoration was not abandoned completely it was certainly sidelined in favour of designs that were either inspired by history (with patterns such as Beardsley or Camelot) or quintessentially English (Wren & Robin or Country Lane). In time various designs were added, with a wide and varied range of gift wares designed by Williamson and Sommerfelt, together with the introduction of bone china to the company's production line.

Table wares flourished under the direction of Elaine Williamson and ranges such as Concert were to prove popular well into the 1990s. Meanwhile, the tradition of external designers providing ideas and inspiration continued with a number of key ranges from leading designers including Robert Welch, John Bromley and Mary Jones Design; however, the most significant relationship of this era was the Queensbury Hunt partnership.

Opposite:
A selection of Beardsley Wares transfer decorated with illustrations from Aubrey Beardsley from designs by Ros Sommerfelt, c. 1979.

An original promotional advertising card for the Vineyard range designed by Anita Harris, c. 1993.

Their Flair and Astral ranges were top-selling table ware designs through the 1980s, and the Calypso and Cello vases added to a secure foundation of development and survival.

The rise of the limited edition and gift market, which had its foundations in the early productions of the 1970s, continued apace led by the expanding range of naturalistic animal studies after designs by Barbara Linley Adams. They were far removed from the daring design-led wares of previous generations yet the collection of naturalistic figures and plates proved popular with the buying public, allowing an opportunity to build a collection.

By the close of the 1980s there was a sense that the worst had passed. The overall improving economic climate in the world was transferred to the everyday running of many companies and Poole Pottery was no exception. With a renewed sense of financial freedom another new direction was once more put into play with the introduction of a fresh modern range, a risk deemed acceptable in the revived market. 'Dorset Fruit', designed by Alan Clarke in 1990, was perfectly pitched for the new 'homely' interior style that was rising to popularity. Inspired by the work of external designers Hinchcliffe and Barber, which had been introduced a few years earlier, the designs utilised a sponge decorating process. This simple yet highly effective method of decoration was to prove a catalyst for numerous other designs, marking yet another successful period for Poole Pottery.

The year 1992 was to prove a landmark once more as the company underwent a series of dramatic developments that would set its fate into the new millennium. In October of that year, Peter Mills led a management buy-out where control of Poole Pottery was taken out of the hands of BTR, the parent firm of Pilkington's. The goal was to build a firm with a future based on its past. At the same time Lord David Queensbury was appointed as Art Director, a move that marked a creative explosion. Queensbury brought many new talents to the table including such important artists as Sarah Chalmers, Kate Byrne and Anita Harris.

A more focused approach was developed regarding future markets and international development. Soon Poole Pottery was one of Britain's leading international exporters with over 50 per cent of the company's production being exported, predominantly to North America and the Far East. Their ability to respond quickly to trends and, more significantly, the new mood in dining, allowed the company to flourish, and during the 1990s there were some striking success stories. Patterns such as 'Vineyard' and 'Vincent' were a huge success while 'Omega', 'Fresco' and 'Terracotta' revived traditional techniques interpreted in a modern and original way. Poole landed pivotal contracts with leading high street firms including John Lewis, Laura Ashley, Heal's and Harrods, while in America it was to be Tiffany's.

With fortunes most definitely on the rise the company drew a great deal of comfort and inspiration from the heritage of Poole's large and accomplished design history. The introduction of a number of new designs that used tried and tested techniques and patterns may have led in some part to the establishment of a new Poole Studio.

Formed in 1995 with Sally Tuffin at the helm, a range was developed with a collection of designs by both in-house and invited artists including Sir Terry Frost, Janice Tchalenko, Charlotte Mellis and, of course, Tuffin herself.

It was Tuffin's contribution which was to prove the most significant. An accomplished and talented designer, Sally Tuffin's intuitive flair saw a stream of new designs including the mainline ranges Seagull, Bird and Fish together with a series of limited editions made exclusively for the newly formed Poole Pottery Collectors' Club, including Strolling Leopard, Forest Deer, Yaffle and Parasol.

In particular it was one design that was to be uniquely important for both Tuffin and Poole Pottery. Her 'Blue Poole' design was selected for what Peter Mills called the 'biggest coup of the year' when British Airways chose it as one of fifteen exclusive motifs created by international artists to adorn the tailfins of their aircraft. In addition, it was to feature across a range of stationery, wallets and other merchandise, taking the Poole style and name around the world.

The newly developed Poole Studio enjoyed further success in the form of Karen Brown's Isle of Purbeck range, which included the immensely

A Seagull pattern charger after designs by Sally Tuffin, c. 1996.

popular Old Harry Rocks and Corfe Castle patterns. Stylistically her work was very much in the manner of Truda Carter and yet again supported the continuing ethos of looking back to move forward.

As the new millennium drew ever closer, once more Poole Pottery dipped into its illustrious design heritage with a range inspired by the vibrant wares of the post-war era. While reminiscent, the new range was most definitely a progression from this earlier style with a fresh selection of colours and more importantly a new way of applying and firing them. Both Alan Clarke and Anita Harris enthusiastically worked with the newly developed glazes created by Yvonne Morris introducing Aurora, Volcano, Galaxy, Clouds, Blue Storm and Odyssey. Launched at Birmingham's National Exhibition Centre's Spring Fair of 1999, the Living Glaze range was an

A limited edition shallow circular charger decorated in the 'Viking' pattern designed by Karen Brown for the Isle of Purbeck series, c. 1998.

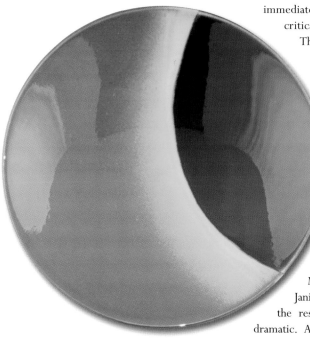

immediate success, sparking orders and critical acclaim in equal measure. The instant response from the market must have echoed the response to Delphis, the range's inspiration, some thirty years earlier.

Keen to push the boundaries, this new glaze was put through its paces with a series of more experimental designs enhancing the limits of the newly developed processes. From in-house designers Anita Harris, Alan Clarke and Nicola Massarella to external artists Janice Tchalenko and Tony Morris, the results were both exciting and dramatic. All the artists produced very different results from the same technical possibilities, but as a combined range the effect was immediate and extraordinary.

Tchalenko's work was more fluid, even organic, while Morris worked in a more painterly approach with abstracted forms or designs based in nature. Alan Clarke developed a range of limited edition plaques for the millennium based on the planets. The work of the new Poole Studio once more underlined the company's position as a market leader and trendsetter and once again had correctly judged the mood of the buying market.

As the world moved towards the new millennium it became apparent that change was yet again on the cards for Poole Pottery. Major development plans were announced which would see a radical transformation of the town of Poole. Plans for a marina in the harbour included the full redevelopment of the Poole Pottery site, which would also include retail and residential accommodation.

As owners of the quayside site the company itself was integral in the relocation plans. Described as the St Tropez of the South Coast, the scheme was finally passed, with work commencing on the site in 2000. The process, costing some £3 million, saw relocation to an industrial site located at Sopers Lane on the outskirts of Poole. The ceasing of production at the old site was marked with the creation of a special limited edition plaque created by Alan Clarke. Once empty, the site including the old factory buildings,

A shallow circular dish form charger decorated in the 'Eclipse' pattern designed by Alan Clarke for the eclipse event that occurred on 11 August 1999.

tearooms, museum and ancillary buildings were demolished, marking the end of 128 years of manufacturing on the same spot.

With the move came a further restructuring in the boardroom. Peter Mills stepped down to concentrate on the property development and his replacement was Chris Rhodes. New ranges were created and as ever external artists were invited to contribute new ideas and ranges, including a series of pieces from Uri Geller.

Despite a positive view and a seemingly strong product range the company fell into difficulties over the course of 2003 and the administrators were called in. The company was sold as a going concern to Dorset businessman Peter Ford, who sought to raise much-needed funds through the sale of the archive at auction, stripping the company of the last vestiges of its heritage.

On 15 December 2006 it was announced that the shop would close, due to non-payment of debts mounting up since the new owners took over in August. The company, including the factory, went into administration on 20 December 2006, owing over £1 million to some 300 creditors. Poole Pottery came out of administration on 10 February 2007 and is now under the control of Lifestyle Group Ltd, which also owns Royal Stafford Tableware.

The pottery shop remains open on Poole Quay, selling Poole Pottery gift ware, lighting, table ware and studio ranges. There is also a studio on site, where Alan White and his team of artists do a large amount of design work for new and future products together with the creation of limited edition and one-off pieces. Sadly the production of Poole Pottery is now undertaken in Burslem, Stoke-on-Trent, such a long way from its ancestral home.

The fact that Poole Pottery still exists is in no small part down to the long and colourful history of this ceramic giant. Over the years there have been a multitude of managers, countless ranges and many great products, all of which contribute to a heritage that is extremely difficult to beat. With the pottery no longer made in sight of the sea, I hope and believe that Poole has the strength to continue building its lasting legacy for another hundred years and more.

A contemporary purse-shaped vase from the Living Glaze range.

INDEX

*Page numbers in italics refer to
illustrations*